D1644524

CITY CYCLING
AMSTERDAM

Rapha.

Thames & Hudson

Created by Andrew Edwards and Max Leonard of
Tandem London, a design, print and editorial studio

Thanks to Joost Stokhof for illustrations; Alex
Figueira for city information; Frank van der Sman for
racing history; and Emile Wilmar and Matt Fee for
bike shops and routes

First published in the United Kingdom in 2013 by
Thames & Hudson Ltd, 181A High Holborn, London WC1V 7QX

City Cycling Amsterdam © 2013 Andrew Edwards and Max Leonard
Illustrations © 2013 Thames & Hudson Ltd, London and Rapha Racing Ltd

Designed by Andrew Edwards

Illustrations by Joost Stokhof, thethingsweare.com

All Rights Reserved. No part of this publication may be reproduced
or transmitted in any form or by any means, electronic or mechanical,
including photocopy, recording or any other information storage and
retrieval system, without prior permission in writing from the publisher.

British Library Cataloguing-in-Publication Data
A catalogue record for this book is available from the British Library

ISBN 978-0-500-29103-0

Printed and bound in China by Everbest Printing Co Ltd

To find out about all our publications, please visit
www.thamesandhudson.com. There you can subscribe
to our e-newsletter, browse or download our current catalogue,
and buy any titles that are in print.

CONTENTS

HOW TO USE THIS GUIDE

This Amsterdam volume of the *City Cycling* series is designed to give you the confidence to explore the city by bike at your own pace. On the front flaps is a locator map of the whole city to help you orient yourself. We've divided the city up into four different neighbourhoods: Centraal (p. 10); West and Vondelpark (p. 18); Oost (p. 24); and Noord (p. 30). All are easily accessible by bike, and are full of cafés, bars, galleries, museums, shops and parks. Each area is mapped in detail, and our recommendations for places of interest and where to fuel up on coffee and cake, as well as where to find a Wi-Fi connection, are marked. Take a pootle round on your bike and see what suits you.

The neighbourhood maps also show bike routes, bike shops and landmarks – everything you need to navigate safely and pinpoint specific locations across a large section of the centre of town. If you fancy a set itinerary, turn to A Day On The Bike, also on the front flaps. It takes you on a relaxed 35km (22-mile) route through some of the parts of Amsterdam we haven't featured in the neighbourhood sections, and visits some of the more touristy sights. Pick and choose the bits you fancy, go from back to front, and use the route as it suits you.

A section on Racing and Training (p. 36) fills you in on some of Amsterdam's cycling heritage and provides ideas for longer rides if you want to explore the beautiful countryside around the city, while Essential Bike Info (p. 40) discusses road etiquette and the ins and outs of navigating your way along Amsterdam's cycle routes. Finally, Links and Addresses (p. 44) will give you the practical details you need to know.

AMSTERDAM:
THE CYCLING CITY

Think Amsterdam, and the image that pops most readily to mind is sure to be one of a bicycle, a bridge and a canal. Everybody – and we mean everybody – cycles in Amsterdam. To experience the city like a local, a bike is essential; it's by far the most convenient and fun way to get around. The beautiful streets of tall, narrow houses are perfect to explore by bike; in fact, the whole city is something of a two-wheeled playground. This is in part thanks to the famous Dutch tolerance, which persisted through religious wars and Nazi occupation, and even today shapes the city. Much of Amsterdam's wealth from the sixteenth-century onwards stems from merchants fleeing Antwerp (then Europe's largest and richest port) after Spain's armies made it clear that Protestants were no longer welcome. They established themselves in Amsterdam, the Dutch East India Company was founded (along with the world's first stock exchange) and the money started pouring in. This was the 'Golden Age', and the city's planners developed the town around four concentric semicircular canals in the Amstel and IJ rivers. They built the bridges between the ninety islands over the 100km (62 miles) of canals, and a compact system of interlocking roads that suits two wheels so much better than four.

Though it might seem as though the Dutch learn to ride a bike before they can walk, the city's bike-friendliness waned after the Second World War. Until 1955, 75 per cent of journeys in town were undertaken by bike, but even Holland was not immune to the spread of the motorcar, and traffic increased. Planners responded by creating larger roads and paving over canals; by the 1970s, the number of journeys by bike had fallen to 25 per cent. Amsterdam's residents fought back, campaigning particularly hard over the many deaths of children caused by cars. In time, the council began to prioritize the reduction of car use, increased road safety and the preservation of the historic town, and slowly the city was transformed. Bike lanes, bike stands and other infrastructure were (and continue to be) built, including the 'main bicycle network', a system of bike lanes so comprehensive that commuting cyclists rarely share road space with fast cars.

These days, bike use is at 35 per cent, though it seems more, and the bicycle is definitely top of the food chain. In the Netherlands, cycling is an almost classless form of transport. People cycle mainly on cheap, heavy upright bikes, usually with one gear and a coaster brake, perfect for the flat terrain. Kids travelling to school ride in the front of their mums' distinctive Bakfiets cargo bikes, often tucked up with a blanket in winter, or sit in a child seat on the top tube. Businessmen cycle to work in suits and ties, women cycle to parties in their evening dresses, friends share their bike or cycle side by side, chatting as they go. People talk on the phone, kiss, laugh, do everything on their bikes. For Amsterdamers, cycling is fun, and it is remarkable how quiet and pleasant a city with little car use is. Generally, cars cede their place to foot and pedal traffic, and drivers are courteous to other road users' needs. The use of cars is discouraged by high parking prices and a complex system of one-way roads (most of which you're allowed to cycle in both directions), which means that for many journeys it's quicker and more convenient to go by bike.

You may think you know Amsterdam, but a bike is the best way of discovering more about the city. You can ride from picture-postcard canals to cutting-edge modern architecture, from dockland regeneration to garden villages in 15 minutes. And there's always something to see: roads turn into paths, footbridges and floating pontoons; huge barges slide into narrow canals at alarmingly high speed; ornate brickwork and tiles decorate the buildings; and there are objets d'art on windowsills and balconies, flowerpots on the steps and art installations in the streets. The air smells of the sea, given the right wind, and the buddleia leaves fall in the spring. Read on to discover the best of what Amsterdam has to offer by bicycle.

NEIGHBOURHOODS

CENTRAAL

MUSEUMS, CANALS AND SEVENTEENTH-CENTURY BEAUTY

Amsterdam's centre encompasses everything that comes to mind when you think of the city, from the tranquil waterside streets of the *Grachtengordel*, semicircular concentric rings of canals that are now a UNESCO World Heritage Site, to the red-light district and coffee shops galore. Our advice is to steer clear of these latter bits while on the bike. The north–south streets in the very centre of Amsterdam around <u>Dam Square</u> are crowded with tourists and trams (not to mention horse-drawn carts), and the cross streets between them are often one way, or prohibited for bikes. De Wallen, or Rossebuurt, as locals know the main red-light district, centred around the canal east of <u>Damrak</u>, is crowded and sleazy, and, while the architecture is lovely, isn't one for riding around. **De Oude Kerk** ①, in the middle, is a beautiful church known for its exhibitions, such as the World Press Photo in the spring, and is perhaps worth a look.

Outside the core, the cycling is lovely and relaxed, with bike lanes galore (only <u>Leidseplein</u> in the southwest seems crowded by trams). A few hundred metres to the east is the Nieuwmarkt neighbourhood, where, above and below the main market square, are picturesque residential roads along the canals. On Saturdays, you'll find the organic **Nieuwmarkt farmers' market** ②, but that hardly disturbs the peace. Nieuwmarkt is in the northeastern corner of Centraal, which is bounded by the Singelgracht canal to the west and south, the Amstel river to the east and the IJ to the north. This is where you'll find **Amsterdam Centraal station** ③ and the tourist office. Further north, on islands jutting out into the water, are the **Openbare Bibliotheek Amsterdam** ④, a huge public library with Wi-Fi, and a seventh-floor restaurant with amazing views. There's also **NEMO** ⑤, a kid-friendly science museum in a shimmering Renzo Piano-designed building. It's fun cycling out over the pontoons past floating restaurants, and if it's the end of the day, grabbing a beer to watch the sun go down with locals at the lively, ramshackle bar and restaurant **Hanneke's Boom** ⑥.

Heading south again, **Waterlooplein flea market** ⑦ is the city's tackiest and most commercial market. It's worth a peep as you cycle past, but the flagship store for **Droog** ⑧, showcasing the design house's own products and a carefully curated selection from around the world, is a must. From here, take the beautiful <u>Prinsengracht</u> or <u>Herengracht</u> canalside streets west. They arc right around the centre, and their stately townhouses are now as likely to house design or ad

agencies as Amsterdam's great and good. Stop off at **Rush Hour** ⑨, one of Holland's most respected record shops, or nearby **Athenaeum Boekhandel** ⑩, a treasure-trove of art, graphic design and foreign-language books and magazines. **Recycled Bicycles** ⑪, one of our recommendations for bicycle hire, is up the road, and for more serious design-book pleasures, head to **Idea Books** ⑫, while photography books are on sale at **Foam** ⑬, Amsterdam's photography museum.

On the west side of town, nestled between the canals, are the famous **Negen Straatjes** ⑭, nine streets of smart shopping boutiques (fashionable streetwear including denim shop **Tenue de Nîmes** ⑮, homeware, antiques, gifts and oddments) and where you'll also find any number of cafés to grab a bite to eat (try **Lust** ⑯ or **Envy** ⑰). Further up Herengracht is the **Anne Frank House** ⑱, where Anne and her family hid from the Nazis, and which now contains a moving museum. It's not far from the floating **Bloemenmarkt** ⑲, where you can buy tulip bulbs for the garden – but don't get that far north without exploring the Jordaan. You'd never know that this was once a working-class district, the scene of dockers' riots in the 1940s. Today its narrow, picture-postcard streets are full of vintage boutiques, small galleries and ateliers. Check out **Back Beat** ⑳ for records, **Sourced and Sold** ㉑ for salvage fixtures and furniture, and

SMBA ㉒, the Stedelijk Museum's project space, which features art, design and digital media. Finally, on the northern boundaries of the Jordaan, is **Moooi** ㉓, which sells lighting, furniture and accessories.

REFUELLING

FOOD	DRINK
The Pancake Bakery is a tourist favourite ㉔	Café Brecht, a hip, relaxed café-cum-bar ㉖
Raïnaraï is a delicious caterer with Middle Eastern specialities ㉕	Two For Joy, the best coffee in town? ㉗

WI-FI
De Bijenkorf, the famous department store, has a café with cake, coffee and Wi-Fi ㉘

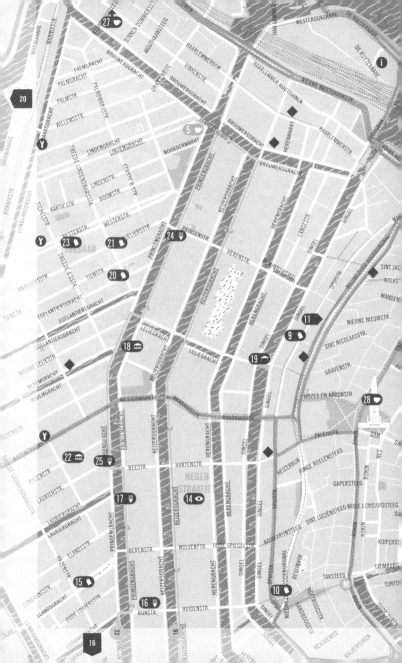

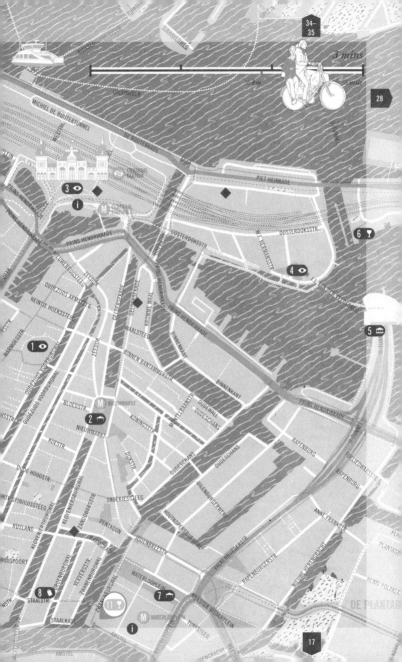

LUNBANSGRACHT
ELANDSGRACHT
OUD...
RACHT

RUNSTR.
HUIDENSTR.

PRINS...
KEI..
HEI..
NIEUWEZIJDS
SANDBOOGSTR.
HOGEBOOG..

LOOIERSGRACHT
LOOIERSGRACHT

PRINSENGR. 14

KEIZERSGR.

14

SINGEL

HEILIGEWEG
KALVERTOREN

PASSEERDERSGRACHT
PASSEERDERSGRACHT
PASSEERDERSGRACHT

LEIDSEGRACHT

LEIDSEGRACHT

HERENGRACHT

KONINGSPLEIN

SINGEL

SINGI

RAAMSTR.

MOLENPAD

LEIDSEGRACHT

LEIDSEGRACHT

REGULIERSDWARSSTR.

LEIDSEGRACHT
LEIDSEGRACHT

KERKSTR.

LEIDSEPLEIN

LEIDSEPLEIN

KEIZERSGRACHT

HERENGRACHT

KEIZERSGRACHT

LEIDSEKADE
MARNIXSTR.

PRINSENGRACHT

PRINSENGRACHT

LUNBAANSGRACHT

LEIDSEPLEIN

LANGE LEIDSEDWARSSTR.

KERKSTR.

SPIEGELKWARTIER

NASSAUKADE

LEIDSEKADE

KORTE LEIDSEDWARSSTR.

PRINSENGRACHT

NIEUWE SPIEGELSTR.

ELMEASTR.

IR..

STADHOUDERSKADE

HIRSCHPASSAGE

PRINSENGRACHT

OVERLOOM

VONDELSTR.

ZIESENISKADE

WETERINGSCHANS

TWEEDE WETERINGDWARSSTR.

ROEMER VISSCHERSTR.

VOSSIUSSTR.

HOBBEMASTR.

STADHOUDERSKADE

WETERINGSCHANS

VIJZELGRACHT

26

P.C. HOOFTSTR.

MUSEUMSTR.

KROMELPAD

TE WTSOEN

PC. HOOFTSTR.

JAN LUUKENSTR.

PAULUS POTTERSTR.

HOBBEMASTR.

WETERINGLAAN

VAN BAERLESTR.

ALEXANDER BOERSSTR.

MUSEUMPLEIN

3

HONTHORSTSTR.

ROYSDAELKADE

EERSTE JACOB VAN CAMPE

22

WILLEMSPARKWEG

RUYSDAELKADE

EFFROLAND ROLSTR.

HOBBEMAKADE

QUELLIJNSTR.

PALESTRINASTR.

MUSEUMKWARTIER

TENIERSSTR.

DANIEL STALPERTSTR.

GABRIEL METSUSTR.

3 mins

½ km

½ mile

WEST & VONDELPARK

FOR LAZY DAYS IN THE PARK AND HIP NIGHTS OUT

Amsterdam's West is a mainly residential district, but within it are many contrasts. Our West area includes some of the opulent Oud Zuid south of the **Vondelpark** ①, Amsterdam's biggest and most famous park, and extends in a strip up through the Oud West almost to the IJ in the north. The grand houses and wide avenues of the Oud Zuid are a good place to start your tour, so we'll cycle this one from south to north. If it's sunny, check out the open-air **Vondelpark Openluchttheater** ②, which hosts bands and cabarets

during the summer and gets very busy at the weekends. Just north of the park is <u>Overtoom</u>, a bustling shopping street with some stand-out shops, including **Pied à Terre** ③, one of the world's biggest travel bookshops, which also houses a café, and **Ari Vintage** ④, a disorderly Aladdin's cave of cheap vintage items. **Abyssinia Afrikaans Eetcafé** ⑤ is Amsterdam's best African restaurant, serving delicious Ethiopian food, while **OT301** ⑥ is an alternative cultural centre, with exhibitions, ateliers and a bar that serves food.

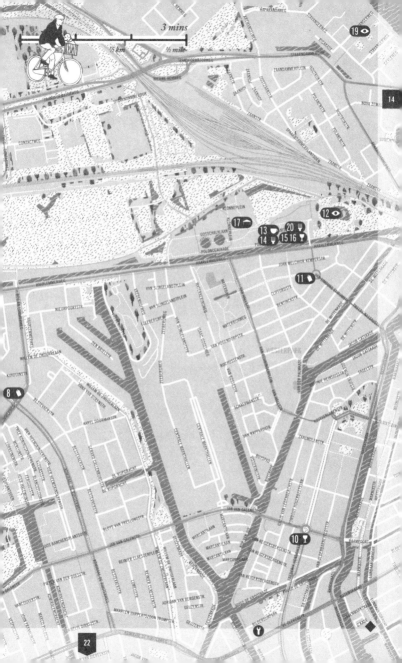

For something more upscale, try **Caffe Oslo** ⑦ at the western end of the street, or **331 West** ⑧ further north, which combines vintage designer clothes with good coffee, and is also a dealer for the city's distinctive Vanmoof bikes. Or, at the other end of Overtoom, **Pristine** ⑨ is Amsterdam's fixed-gear boutique. It's filled with shiny new bikes, vintage bits, magazines and photography, and the staff are friendly and helpful. Riding up through Oud West, you pass through blocks of large, handsome residential buildings, with children's playgrounds on the quiet streets. **De Nieuwe Anita** ⑩ is a hip bar with a cosy atmosphere, while **Hippo Vintage** ⑪ is on a quiet back street, and sells interesting lighting and chairs.

Until you get to **Westerpark** ⑫, there's not much green space in this part of the West (though if you head further out, there's Rembrantpark and Erasmuspark). Next to the park and the canal is Cultuurpark Westergasfabriek, a cultural development on the site of a former gas works, now home to cafés, restaurants and music venues. For a seriously strong coffee, go to Espressofabriek ⑬. **Pacific Parc** ⑭ is a restaurant that turns into a club after dinner, and the **North Sea Jazz Club** ⑮ and **Toko MC** ⑯ host contemporary local and international jazz, electronic and urban music talent. The area's rows of industrial buildings also make for an interesting afternoon stroll.

The **Sunday Market** ⑰ (first Sunday of the month, for crafts, kids stuff and art) and **Ten Katemarkt** ⑱ (Mondays–Saturdays, for fresh food and lunch stalls) are also nearby. If that all sounds too busy, why not head to **Strand West** ⑲ (on Stavangerweg). The huge beach with panoramic views of the IJ is popular with Amsterdam's youth. But be warned: Saturday afternoon relaxing can easily turn into Saturday evening cocktails and dancing.

REFUELLING

FOOD	DRINK
De Bakkerswinkel ⑳ at the entrance to the Cultuurpark Westergasfabriek	Het Blauwe Theehuis ㉑ is a hip café in the Vondelpark

WI-FI
Espressofabriek ⑬ has free Wi-Fi and outside tables

OOST

Oost as featured here covers a huge area of Amsterdam, taking you from the inner city just outside its watery girdle, along the IJ to converted docklands (now that port traffic has moved west), and down into the heart of the Oost neighbourhood – multicultural, vibrant and slightly shabby in places – right to the fringes of tranquil Watergrafsmeer in the south. Essentially, we're talking everything east of the Amstel River. Closest to the city centre, don't miss the **Resistance Museum** ①, on a quiet corner of the Plantage, which tells the story of how the Dutch fought the German occupation during the Second World War. Close by are **Kriterion** ②, a cinema and bar, and the **Tropenmuseum** ③, an impressive anthropological museum with a theatre that is the best world-music venue in town. It's all very close to the main university buildings, and to **CREA** ④, the university's cultural centre, which hosts theatre, live music, lectures and debates that are open to all.

Heading north, to the old docks on the IJ, the first stop is the **Bimhuis** ⑤, the new incarnation of the classic jazz venue. It has audiences queuing up to watch jazz greats perform on the glass-backed stage, with trains and cars passing behind. Further along is **Pakhuis Wilhelmina** ⑥, one of the most progressive club and music venues in the city. East again is **Odessa** ⑦, a restaurant in a Ukrainian fishing boat that serves good food in 1970s lounge surroundings. It's near the bridge to **KNSM-eiland** ⑧, a reclaimed island and former steamboat dock, where you'll find modern design and homeware shops, including the excellently named **Pols Potten** ⑨, which sells, yes, pots.

The whole of the east is full of shipping history. **Theater Fabriek** ⑩ occupies an old ship engine factory, and puts on contemporary and avant-garde shows. Or find your way through car parks and a trading estate to converted warehouse **Roest** ⑪, and hang out on a canalside beach with quality dance music in the evenings. **Studio/K** ⑫ has a similarly laid-back vibe. For a more traditional Amsterdam experience, head to the **Brouwerij 't IJ** ⑬, a fantastic-looking windmill where they make their own beer. Cross the bridge here, and you're into the Oost neighbourhood proper. Many roads are named after former Dutch colonies, with smart social and private housing. Javastraat is probably the most multicultural street in Amsterdam, a real melting pot. Try **Jansen Vintage** ⑭ for mid-century design and furniture, just behind the **Badhuis Javaplein** ⑮, a former public bathhouse and now a bar with a great wine list and one of the best terraces in the city. Way out east are the **Flevoparkbad outdoor swimming pools** ⑯ if you still fancy a dip. The Flevopark is possibly the most peaceful park in a town full of peaceful parks, and **Camping Zeeburg** ⑰ is an inner-city campsite, with good facilities.

Heading back west, **Dappermarkt** ⑱ is a bustling, multicultural market, the **Oosterpark** ⑲ is an easy-riding park for bikes, and the Eerste Oosterparkstraat is home to Turkish bakeries and traditional Dutch cafés. As you get closer to the river, there are a variety of places to end the day. **Canvas** ⑳ is on the seventh floor of the Volkskrant

building, a former newspaper office now full of artists' studios. The terrace has great views, there's always music, and the *bitterballen* – ham and cheese croquettes – are a great snack to have with beer. **Trouw** ㉑ across the road is the place to go for dance music, but for a more mellow evening, the Amstel dock is a good place to watch the sun go down – where **Hesp** ㉒, a lively locals' 'brown' bar, will serve you Belgian beer and also cooks a decent steak.

REFUELLING

FOOD	DRINK
De Ysbreeker ㉓, a relaxed riverside bar for coffee in the day and beer at night	Beter & Leuk ㉔, a quiet coffee shop

WI-FI
Coffee Company ㉕, which also has branches across town

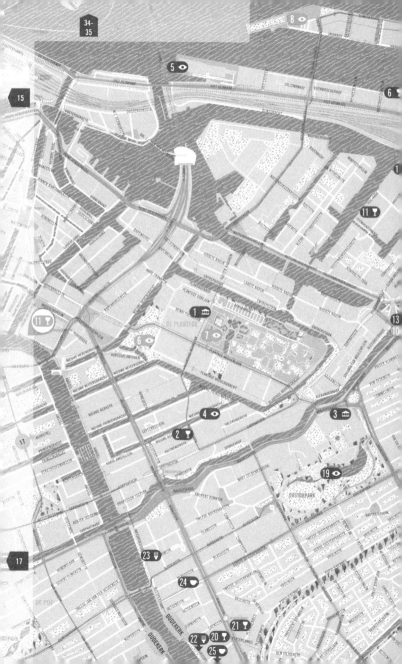

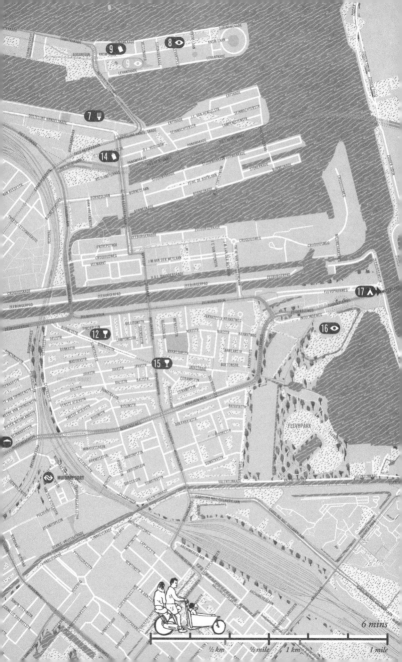

GARDEN VILLAGES AND DOCKLAND REGENERATION

Amsterdam's Noord, which in this guide designates everything across the IJ, on the north bank of the river, is certainly the most varied, and perhaps inspiring, part of town to explore. It's also one whose charms you might miss completely if you weren't on a bike. Amid the industrial estates and out-of-town shops, there's docklands regeneration, arts projects and alternative living, along with beautiful garden villages. To get there, take the free, bike-friendly ferry from behind Centraal station to Buiksloterweg. It's the green line, and the shortest way across, though you can also get ferries from Centraal to NDSM, and from NDSM to Tasmaanstraat in the West.

Immediately obvious is the **EYE Film Institute** ①, the Dutch centre for film culture, housed in a white splinter of a building on

the water. It shows classics in their original language, and is also worth a visit for the astonishing cantilevered terrace. Dining options nearby include the **Tolhuistuin** ②, a new arts complex housed in a former Shell science centre. Move away from the riverfront and ride west, and you're quickly reminded that this side of the river has always meant business. You'll cycle past chemical companies and industrial premises, and eventually reach the monolithic **NDSM** ③, a post-industrial space now used for artists' studios – it's fine to

go inside and take a look around. Once a month, the **IJ-Hallen** ④, Europe's biggest flea market, takes over one of the warehouses. You'll see inventive uses for relics of the shipping trade everywhere. Hunt out the brightly coloured **shipping containers** ⑤ and **old city trams** ⑥ now being used as houses, or the rusting crane next to the colossal slipway. The wide open spaces are made for cruising, and there's impressive modern architecture in the form of office blocks on Kraanspoor. Stop off at alternative café **Noorderlicht** ⑦ to eat organic food surrounded by greenhouses and tomato plants, or relax on the sofas at **Pllek** ⑧, a chilled-out bar, also made from shipping containers, with its own beach and a great view over the IJ.

One of Amsterdam's more bizarre sights is also in the area: a former **Soviet submarine** ⑨, parked in the river. Unsurprisingly, given the creativity in the neighbourhood and the space available, many buildings now house galleries. Things move fast, but try **Nieuw Dakota** ⑩ to start. Another legacy of the shipbuilding industry are Noord's garden villages. Built in the 1910s and '20s for the growing army of workers, these architecturally enlightened housing projects contributed to Amsterdam's reputation for outstanding public housing. The Tuindorp Oostzaan neighbourhood is centred around the pretty **Zonneplein** ⑪, while Tuindorp Nieuwendam and Buiksloot, further out and to the east, are more rural again, incorporating old wooden housing from when the areas were just villages outside Amsterdam. The <u>Nieuwendammerdijk</u> is particularly pretty – all carved and painted wood, beautiful interiors and antiques, it's a waterside idyll. Head out that way over the Willem I lock to <u>Sixhavenweg</u> and take the bike path. Stop off at **Neef Louis** ⑫, possibly the city's best vintage furniture store, which specializes in ex-industrial pieces.

REFUELLING

FOOD	DRINK
Café-Restaurant Stork ⑬ for fish and great waterside seating	Ot en Sien ⑭ is a cosy café with Belgian beers

WIFI
IJ Kantine ⑮ will let you surf for free, and is great for brunch and coffee

RACING AND TRAINING

While the Dutch aren't quite as bike-crazy as the Belgians, the Netherlands is one of cycling's traditional northern European heartlands. Amsterdam's first cycling club was established in 1884; by 1900, there were around sixty, and the first road race (93km [58 miles] from Amsterdam to Arnhem in 1885) was but a distant memory. Between 1905 and 1936, racing on public roads was banned in the Netherlands, so most of the action took place on Amsterdam's numerous local velodromes – first on a cinder track behind the Rijksmuseum, and subsequently on wood and concrete, under cover and in the open air, at several tracks around town.

Notwithstanding the road-racing ban, in 1909 the Olympia cycle club organized the Ronde van Nederland (Tour of the Netherlands); it would become a week-long stage race, which for most of its life started and ended in the capital. Gerrie Knetemann, the Amsterdam-born world champion in 1978, is the most successful rider of the Ronde with four wins. Riding most famously for the Ti-Raleigh team, under fearsome *directeur sportif* Peter Post, Knetemann notched up an impressive ten stage wins at the Tour de France. When the UCI instigated the ProTour in 2005, the race became the Tour du Benelux – even though it has never visited Luxembourg. Other famous pros from Amsterdam include Jaap Eden, who was both cycling and speed-skating world champion in the 1890s, and Gerrit Schulte, who beat Fausto Coppi in 1948 to become World Pursuit Champion.

In 1928, the Olympics visited town (the stadium still survives, though the velodrome is no more). The Dutch won four cycling medals, coming second in the medal table and equalling Denmark's haul, though the Danes won more golds. But Amsterdam's real golden age of cycling came after the Second World War, when each neighbourhood would hold a *wielerronde*. Loosely translating as 'cycling competitions', these were essentially criterium races on closed roads. Between May and September, twenty to twenty-five *rondes* would be held – Indische Buurt, Vondelpark, Albert Cuypstraat and Vismarkt all had one, with the Ronde van Lindengracht being particularly special. Residents would hang out of their windows to watch, with up to ten thousand spectators lining the streets to cheer the riders on. Westerstraat would also host a *kruideniersrace*, or 'grocers' race', in which local tradesmen would do battle on their cargo bikes.

The *wielerrondes* were, unfortunately, a victim of their own success, with the council becoming increasingly unwilling to shut so many roads to cars every weekend, or for organizers to charge a fee. On 1 January 1956, they came largely to an end, and only the Ronde van het Purmerplein in the Noord survives today. In their heyday, the Tour de France also came to town. In 1954, the Dutch capital hosted the *grand départ*, the first time the race had started outside France. In a heated first stage from the **Olympic Stadium**, 216km (134 miles) to Brasschaat, in Belgium, Swiss star Hugo Koblet split the pack, and the Dutch rider Wout Wagtmans won. The Tour has never been back to Amsterdam, but the Giro d'Italia paid a visit in 2010, basing itself in Amsterdam for three days. In the 8.4km (5-mile) first stage, Bradley Wiggins took the *maglia rosa* in his first Grand Tour victory for Team Sky; stage 2 saw Tyler Farrar win the sprint into Utrecht, while Wouter Weylandt won a chaotic stage 3 from Amsterdam to Middelberg.

These days, as far as amateur racing goes, there are only three clubs left in town – **Olympia**, **De Germaan** and **Ulysses** – and to join their training rides you'd really need to be a member. The bike shops **Cycle You** and **Pristine** (p. 21), however, both run weekly rides (and Pristine, the fixed-gear specialists, do ride road bikes on them). For links to racing and training routes, please see our Links and Addresses section, where you can also find details for **Tromm Tweewielers** and **Presto Cycle Sport** – both good bike-shop choices for repairs and spares for serious roadies.

Finally, there's the Amsterdam Six Day race, which opens the annual European Six Day season (it takes place at the end of October, at the **Sloten Velodrome** near Schiphol airport). In between 1932 and 2001, it was only held eight times. Annual since then, it's now one of the larger and more prestigious Sixes on the calendar.

ESSENTIAL BIKE INFO

Cycling in Amsterdam is a way of life, and if you hire an inconspicuous black bike, it's easy to blend in. Locals rarely wear helmets, as cycling in town is so safe and relaxed. Here are a few things to know to help your trip go as smoothly as possible.

ETIQUETTE

There is something of an 'anything goes' attitude to cycling in Amsterdam, and it's remarkable how well all road users co-operate, but there are certain things you can do to respect other cyclists and vehicles on the road. Be courteous and keep your wits about you, and you'll have a ball.

- The cardinal rule in Amsterdam is to always indicate that you're turning before you do. The Dutch expect it, and will not otherwise make allowances for your manoeuvre.
- Always cycle on the right-hand side of the bike lane, so people can overtake you.
- If you're planning on overtaking someone, check over your left shoulder that it's safe to pull out before you do.
- Generally, people will stop at red lights, although they seem less inclined to obey bicycle-specific traffic lights, which you will see frequently in bike lanes.

SAFETY

Amsterdam is very safe on a bike, and cars will unfailingly be aware of your presence. Drivers turning across a segregated bike path will not encroach on your space; this is equally true of cars travelling in the same direction as you and those crossing a bike lane at a junction. There are a few things to watch out for:

- Bikes are often allowed up one-way streets. If there's a 'No Entry' sign, and another sign showing a bicycle and the word *Uitgezonderd*, then it's OK – bikes are excepted.
- Sometimes it can be difficult to see when a bike lane is one way or not. Generally, where the lane is wide enough, other cyclists tolerate people cycling the wrong way. Be careful, however, that the lane doesn't narrow, or integrate with a road without you realizing

- at that point you'll find yourself cycling on the wrong side of the street, with cars and bikes coming towards you.
- Trams act as if they own the road – and you shouldn't argue with them!
- Pay attention to tram lines too, which can trap skinny tyres and become slippery when wet.
- Scooters are allowed in bike lanes, so keep an eye out for them.
- Dutch cyclists are confident and quick (even on their heavy, upright bikes), and are used to cycling in busy cycle lanes. They don't give you much room, and don't take any prisoners! Following the etiquette points above will help keep you out of the way of contretemps with bikes and scooters.
- Use lights after dark – the police disapprove of people who don't. Most Dutch bikes have dynamo lights, so this shouldn't be an issue.
- There are a lot of tourists cycling around: it's likely some of them are novice cyclists and that others, given Amsterdam's 'party-city' reputation and coffee shops, might be a little worse for wear. If you see groups on bright hire bikes, make allowances for them.
- Watch out for horse-drawn carts full of tourists in and around Dam Square.

SECURITY

Amsterdam, like many cities, has a problem with bicycle theft, with some people estimating that 10 per cent of bicycles get stolen. Your hire bike should come with a chain lock, and we recommend using it to tie the bike to something immovable if you're going to leave it unattended (many Amsterdamers simply chain their bike to itself, or use the wheel lock integrated into most frames, but this seems an avoidable risk).

In the centre of town there are so many bikes around it can be difficult to find a railing or bike stand to lock it to, but it's a good idea to do so – and if you've come to town with a valuable bike, it's essential. Think about using two locks, so that opportunist bike thieves will pick an easier target.

FINDING YOUR WAY

There is a good system of signposts on Amsterdam's bike routes, and street signs in the centre are marked with their neighbourhood name (Centrum, Oost, etc). There are also good walking signposts.

When travelling with a purpose, or going longer distances, it pays to take one of the larger, straighter roads, even if it takes you slightly out of your way, and then cut into the smaller roads when you're closer to your destination. This is equally true in the semicircle of the *Grachtengordel* – it's far easier and more pleasant to cycle a half moon around Prinsengracht or Herengracht than cut straight across the middle of Dam Square.

HIRING BIKES

There are a million and one places to hire a bike in Amsterdam. We recommend **StarBikes** and **Recycled Bicycle**s (p. 12), both in the centre of town, for Dutch-bike hire. If you want a road bike, head to **Kaptein Tweewielers**, and for a cyclo-cross bike head to **Beekhoven Bikes**.

OTHER PUBLIC TRANSPORT

Dutch buses and most trams do not accept bikes, though you can take bikes on the IJtram 26 line that runs from Centraal station to the eastern suburbs. You can take bikes on the Metro, but must pay a supplement to do so; the city's free boats, which criss-cross the IJ, linking the Noord to the centre, allow bikes on for free. Purchase a day ticket and you can take a bike on Dutch trains. Tickets are often checked, so don't forget.

TRAVELLING TO AMSTERDAM WITH BIKES

Amsterdam is well served by international trains, which are the safest way to travel with a bike. There are direct services to Paris, Antwerp, Brussels and the major German cities. Cities in Austria and Switzerland connect via Cologne, and you can travel from further afield on sleeper trains.

Eurostar is the most relaxed way to travel to Amsterdam from London: the Eurostar website will sell you a ticket for Amsterdam, changing in Brussels, with the fastest journey currently taking four and a half hours, but as of 2013, bags longer than 85cm (33 in.) are not allowed as carry-on luggage, which practically rules out non-folding bikes. You can – for a fee – reserve a bike space on the train, but on the **Thalys** trains from Brussels to Amsterdam, bicycles must be disassembled and carried in a bag – so in effect you'll have to bag the bike for the Eurostar section, too. That means you must book it a place as registered baggage, which currently costs £10 per journey for the 'Turn Up and Go' service, where you leave your bike at a counter in the check-in hall. Once on the Thalys, the large luggage racks mean the whole business is fairly hassle-free. Two strategies seem to work: either race to the front of the queue to board, so that you can be sure of securing a space in the rack; or, if your bike bag is fairly slimline, wait until everyone else has stowed their luggage, and slide it in on top.

German Intercity-Express (ICE) trains will not allow bike bags bigger than 85cm (33 in.) in any dimension. Intercity (IC) and Eurocity (EC) trains, however, do allow bikes to be wheeled on board if you pay for a reservation, or carried in a regular-sized bag, so it's best to factor in a slow train if you're arriving in Amsterdam from Germany. All trains allow folding bikes, though on ICE trains these must again be bagged.

Amsterdam's **Schiphol airport** is one of the only major European airports you could recommend cycling to and from. It's less than 20km (12 miles) from the centre of town, and you can cycle on signposted bike paths almost all the way. When heading back to the airport, our advice is to get a map, either from the tourist office or from **Pied à Terre** (p. 19), the travel bookshop on Overtoom, so that you don't miss the plane home.

LINKS AND ADDRESSES

Abyssinia Afrikaans Eetcafé
Jan Pieter Heijestraat 190,
1054 MN
abyssinia.nl

Albert Cuyp street market
Albert Cuypstraat 67/HS,
1072 CN
albertcuypmarkt.nl

Anne Frank House
Prinsengracht 267, 1016 GV
annefrank.org

Ari Vintage
Overtoom 532, 1054 LL

Artis Royal Zoo
Plantage Kerklaan 40, 1018 CZ
artis.nl

Athenaeum Boekhandel
Spuistraat 14, 1012 XA
athenaeum.nl

Back Beat
Egelantiersstraat 19, 1015 PV
backbeat.nl

Badhuis Javaplein
Javaplein 21, 1095 CJ
badhuis-javaplein.nl

Bazar
Albert Cuypstraat 182, 1073 BL
bazaramsterdam.nl

Beter & Leuk
Eerste Oosterparkstraat 91,
1091 GW
beterenleuk.nl

Bimhuis
Piet Heinkade 3, 1019 BR
bimhuis.nl

Bloemenmarkt
Singel 610-616, 1017
keesbevaart.nl

Brouwerij 't IJ
Funenkade 7, 1018 AL
brouwerijhetij.nl

Café Brecht
Weteringschans 157, 1017 SE
cafebrecht.nl

Café-Restaurant Stork
Gedempt Hamerkanaal t.o. 96,
1021 KR
restaurantstork.nl

Café Thijssen
Brouwersgracht 107, 1015 GD
cafethijssen.nl

Caffe Oslo
Sloterkade 1 A, 1058 HD
caffeoslo.nl

Camping Zeeburg
Zuider IJdijk 20, 1095 KN
campingzeeburg.nl

Canvas
Wibautstraat 150, 1091 GR
canvas7.nl

Coffee Company
Meester Treublaan 18, 1097 DP
coffeecompany.nl

CREA
Nieuwe Achtergracht 170,
1018 WV
crea.uva.nl

Dappermarkt
Dapperstraat 279, 1093 BS
dappermarkt.nl

De Bijenkorf
Dam 1, 1012 JS
debijenkorf.nl

De Bakkerswinkel
Regulateurshuis 1,
Polonceaukade 1, 1014 DA
debakkerswinkel.com

De Hortus
Plantage Middenlaan 2a,
1018 DD
dehortus.nl

De Nieuwe Anita
Frederik Hendrikstraat 115,
1052 HN
denieuweanita.nl

De Oude Kerk
Oudekerksplein 23, 1012 GX
oudekerk.nl

De Ysbreeker
Weesperzijde 23, 1091 EC
deysbreeker.nl

Droog
Staalstraat 7B, 1011 JJ
droog.com

Espressofabriek
Gosschalklaan 7, 1014 DC
espressofabriek.nl

Envy
Prinsengracht 381, 1016 HL
envy.nl

EYE Film Institute
IJpromenade 1, 1031 KT
eyefilm.nl

Flevoparkbad
Zeeburgerdijk 630, 1095 AN
oost.amsterdam.nl

Foam
Keizersgracht 609, 1017 DS
foam.org

Grand Café Amstelhoeck
Amstel 1, 1011 PN
amstelhoeck.nl

Hanneke's Boom
Dijksgracht 4, 1019 BS
hannekesboom.nl

Hesp
Weesperzijde 131, 1091 ER
cafehesp.nl

Het Blauwe Theehuis
Vondelpark 5, 1071 AA
blauwetheehuis.nl

Hippo Vintage
Van Limburg Stirumplein, 1051

Idea Books
Nieuwe Herengracht 11, 1011 RK
ideabooks.nl

IJ-Hallen
Tt. Neveritaweg 15, 1033 WB
ijhallen.nl

IJ Kantine
Mt. Ondinaweg 15–17, 1033 RE
ijkantine.nl

Jansen Vintage
Javaplein 31hs, 1019 CJ
jansenvintage.nl

Kriterion
Roetersstraat 170, 1018 WE
kriterion.nl

Lust
Runstraat 13, 1016 GJ
lustamsterdam.nl

Moooi
Westerstraat 187, 1015 MA
moooi.com

NDSM
Ms. Van Riemsdijkweg, 1033
ndsm.nl

Neef Louis
Papaverweg 46–48, 1032 KJ
neeflouis.nl

Negen Straatjes
de9straatjes.nl

NEMO
Oosterdok 2, 1011 VX
e-nemo.nl

Nieuw Dakota
Ms. van Riemsdijkweg 41B,
1033 RC
nieuwdakota.com

Nieuwmarkt farmers' market
Nieuwmarkt, 1012 CR
nieuwmarkt.org

Noorderlicht
NDSM Plein 102, 1033 WB
noorderlichtcafe.nl

North Sea Jazz Club
Pazzanistraat 1, 1014 DB
northseajazzclub.com

Odessa
Veemkade 259, 1019 CZ
de-odessa.nl

**Openbare Bibliotheek
Amsterdam**
Oosterdokskade 143, 1011 DL
oba.nl

Ot en Sien
Buiksloterweg 27, 1031 CD

OT301
Overtoom 301, 1054 HW
ot301.nl

Pacific Parc
Polonceaukade 23, 1014 DA
pacificparc.nl

Pakhuis Wilhelmina
Veemkade 576, 1019 BL
cafepakhuiswilhelmina.nl

Pied à Terre
Overtoom 135, 1054 HG
jvw.nl

Pllek
Tt. Neveritaweg 59, 1033 WB
pllek.nl

Pols Potten
KNSM-laan 39, 1019 LA
polspotten.nl

Raïnaraï
Prinsengracht 252, 1016 HG
rainarai.nl

Resistance Museum
Plantage Kerklaan 61A, 1018 CX
verzetsmuseum.org

Roest
Czaar Peterstraat 213b, 1018 PL
amsterdamroest.nl

Rush Hour
Spuistraat 98, 1012 TZ
rushhour.nl

SMBA
Rozenstraat 59, 1016 NN
smba.nl

Sourced and Sold
Eerste Tuindwarsstraat 16,
1015 RV
sourcedandsold.com

Strand West
Stavangerweg 900, 1013 AX
strand-west.nl

Studio/K
Timorplein 62, 1094 CC
studio-k.nu

Sunday Market
Haarlemmerweg 8–10, 1014 BE
sundaymarket.nl

Ten Katemarkt
Ten Katestraat, 1053
detenkatemarkt.nl

Tenue de Nimes
Elandsgracht 60, 1016 TX
tenuedenimes.com

Theater Fabriek
Czaar Peterstraat 213, 1018 PL
theaterfabriekamsterdam.nl

The Pancake Bakery
Prinsengracht 191, 1015 DS
pancake.nl

Toko MC
Polonceaukade 5, 1014 DA
tokomc.nl

Tolhuistuin
Tolhuisweg 5, 1031 CL
tolhuistuin.nl

Tropenmuseum
Linnaeusstraat 2, 1092 CK
tropenmuseum.nl

Trouw
Wibautstraat 131, 1091 GL
trouwamsterdam.nl

Two For Joy
Frederiksplein 29, 1017 XL
twoforjoy.nl

Vondelpark Openluchttheater
Vondelpark 5a, 1071 AA
openluchttheater.nl

Waterlooplein flea market
Waterlooplein, 1011 PG
waterloopleinmarkt.nl

BIKE SHOPS, CLUBS, RACES AND VENUES

For links to our racing and training routes, please visit **citycyclingguides.com**

Beekhoven Bikes
Draaierweg 16, 1032 KS
beekhovenbikes.nl

Cycle You
Schellingwouderdijk 339, 1023 NK
cycleyou.nl

De Germaan
Bok de Korverweg 8, 1067 HR
asvdegermaan.bekijknu.nl

Kaptein Tweewielers
Overtoom 488-490, 1054 JZ
kapteintweewielers.nl

Olympia
Sloterweg 1045, 1006 AD
ascolympia.nl

Olympic Stadium
Olympisch Stadion 2, 1076 DE
olympischstadion.nl

Presto Cycle Sport
Haarlemmerstraat 76, 1013 ET
presto.nl

Pristine
Kinkerstraat 14, 1053 DV
pristinefixedgear.com

Recycled Bicycles
Spuistraat 84A, 1012 TX
recycledbicycles.org

Sloten Velodrome
Sloterweg 1045, 1066 CD
velodrome.nl

StarBikes
De Ruyterkade 127, 1011 AC
starbikesrental.com

331 West
Admiraal de Ruijterweg 331, 1055 LZ
331west.nl

Tromm Tweewielers
Europaplein 45, 1078 GV
tromm.nl

Ulysses
Beemsterstraat 654, 1027 ED
arc-ulysses.nl

OTHER USEFUL SITES

Amsterdam Centraal Station
Stationsplein 9, 1012 A
amsterdamcentraal.nu

Eurostar
eurostar.com

Schiphol Airport
Evert v/d Beekstraat 202, 1118 CP Schiphol
schiphol.nl

Thalys
thalys.com

Rapha, established in London, has always been a champion of city cycling – from testing our first prototype jackets on the backs of bike couriers, to a whole range of products designed specifically for the demands of daily life on the bike. As well as an online emporium of products, films, photography and stories, Rapha has a growing network of Cycle Clubs, locations around the globe where cyclists can enjoy live racing, food, drink and products. Rapha is also the official clothing supplier of Team Sky, the world's leading cycling team.

Rapha.